A Story of Courage: Supreme Court Justice Sonia Sotomayor

Dr. Dolores T. Burton

and

Dr. Patricia Ann Marcellino

A Story of Courage: Supreme Court Justice Sonia Sotomayor describes the story of a Hispanic girl from the Bronx in New York City, who had a dream to become a lawyer and a judge. The Justice's story is an example of how courage and perseverance can be used to overcome challenges against all odds.

Copyright

Dedications

From Dr. Dolores T. Burton:

This book is dedicated to my husband, Bernard. Whenever I had doubts, he encouraged me to "Just Do It!" and to my grandchildren Nicholas and Jennifer who possess many of the same characteristics as Justice Sotomayor.

From Dr. Patricia Ann Marcellino:

This book is dedicated to my husband, Carl; my Uncle Nicolo (who introduced me to the power and joy of reading); my son Carl Philip; my daughter Jean Patricia; my son-in-law Joseph Peter; and my grandchildren, Aleia Ann and Robert Carl.

About The Book

Dreams can come true. This book tells the story of the vision, dreams, and courage of Supreme Court Justice Sonia Maria Sotomayor. Justice Sotomayor is one of nine Justices, who decide cases by interpreting the laws based on the Constitution of the United States of America. Her job makes her a very powerful person because she sits on the highest court in the land. The story begins when Sonia was a child, and she first dreamed about who she would become when she grew up. As a young girl, Sonia dreamed of becoming a lawyer and a judge. She worked hard in school, and throughout her career as a lawyer and a judge, she always tried to do her very best. In spite of the obstacles that stood in her way, Sonia persevered with courage and determination and fulfilled her dreams. Supreme Court Justice Sonia Sotomayor's life serves as an example to every girl and boy that dreams can be achieved, and with courage and bravery, every life can be a dream come true.

Table of Contents

CHAPTER 1...1

CHAPTER 2...5

CHAPTER 3..11

CHAPTER 4..17

CHAPTER 5..21

CHAPTER 6..27

CHAPTER 7..33

CHAPTER 8..39

CHAPTER 9 43

CHAPTER 10 49

CHAPTER 11 55

CHAPTER 12 63

CHAPTER 13 73

UNITED STATES COURT SYSTEMS.............83

WORDS TO KNOW..89

LEGAL TERMS GLOSSARY 91

VIDEOS ABOUT JUSTICE SOTOMAYOR....97

OTHER WEBSITES...103

REFERENCES 107

TEACHER RESOURCES 113

COMMON CORE STATE STANDARDS.......115

ABOUT THE AUTHORS...................................121

CHAPTER 1

Growing Up in the 1950s and 1960s

"Don't ever stop dreaming. Don't ever stop trying. There's courage in trying."
Justice Sonia Sotomayor

Vision is the ability to dream about what could be. Courage is the ability to follow that dream despite barriers and difficulties. Sonia had vision and courage. Like many girls growing up in the 1950s, the books she read and the TV shows she watched influenced her. Her favorite books were the *Nancy Drew Mystery Stories*. Nancy was smart and courageous. She could solve a mystery no matter where it took place. Nancy solved mysteries by looking for clues. Whatever the mystery, Nancy could solve it. When Sonia was a child, her dream was to become a detective and solve mysteries just like *Nancy Drew*.

Sonia's favorite TV show in the 1960s was a story about a fictional Los Angeles criminal defense lawyer named *Perry Mason*. Perry questioned witnesses in court, and he would often be able to figure out the truth from the lies of the witnesses. On each TV show, because of his excellent questions, he found the guilty person.

Even though Perry was a lawyer, he sometimes acted like a detective. He was able to find the real thief or murderer from their answers to his questions. When the charges against the defendant, Perry's client, were dropped, the real criminal was arrested and taken away in handcuffs. Because he solved crimes, *Perry Mason* reminded Sonia of *Nancy Drew*. He became part of her vision and her dream.

Sonia knew she would make a great

detective. She was brave, a good listener, and she liked to question people. She also enjoyed solving puzzles, looking for clues, and figuring things out like *Nancy Drew* and *Perry Mason*. Even though *Nancy Drew* and *Perry Mason* were not real people, when Sonia was a child, she studied what they did and learned from them.

CHAPTER 2

Sonia Was a Lively and Helpful Child

Sonia was the first child in her family to be born on the mainland of the United States of America. Her parents, Celina and Juan, came to New York City from Puerto Rico during World War II in the 1940s. Her mother, who Sonia called Mami, first worked as a hospital telephone operator, and then later she worked as a nurse. Her father, who Sonia called Papi, worked as a tool and die worker in a factory. Papi insisted that only Spanish, not English, be spoken in their home.

When Sonia was a child, Mami worked at night and Papi worked during the day. Each night Papi cooked dinner for Sonia and her younger brother, Juan. Sonia was three years older than Juan who was named after his father. He was nicknamed Junior.

After school on Friday afternoons, Sonia went with Papi to the *bodega*, a local grocery store. She helped him shop for food, while one of their neighbors watched

Junior. Shopping for food was Papi and Sonia's special private time together.

Sonia protected her brother from the bullies on the playground. However, like some big sisters, she was also a bit bossy with Junior. Sometimes she even played jokes on Junior.

Both children always obeyed their father's rules. Papi had a rule that they were not allowed to invite friends over to their apartment after school. Because of this rule, Sonia and Junior spent a lot of their time together doing their homework, reading books, and watching TV.

Weekends were fun for Sonia and Junior. They played with their cousins at their grandmother's apartment. Their grandmother, Abuelita, lived only a few short blocks from Sonia and Junior. Abuelita was Papi's mother. Papi's sisters, Sonia's and Junior's aunts, also lived nearby. The aunts also brought their children, Sonia's cousins, to Abuelita's apartment on Saturday nights. Sonia and Junior enjoyed playing with their four cousins: Eddie, Miriam, Nelson, and Lillian. Their four cousins were also their best friends.

At Abuelita's, everyone dressed up, danced, sang, and played musical instruments. Sometimes they played games like *BINGO*. On some Saturday nights, Sonia, Junior, and their four cousins slept at Abuelita's apartment. The fun always continued into the Sunday morning hours.

Sonia loved Abuelita and her aunts. They were pretty and always happy. They were Sonia's real live heroines and her earliest role models. She learned from them just like she learned from *Nancy Drew* and *Perry Mason*.

CHAPTER 3

Sonia's Dream Changes

At seven years old, Sonia learned that she could not become a detective. After a medical examination, a doctor told Sonia's parents that she had diabetes. The doctor gave Sonia a brochure that explained everything about diabetes. In it was a list of jobs that people with diabetes could not do. The list included the jobs of police officer and detective. These jobs required passing a medical examination. Since Sonia had diabetes, she would not be able to pass the medical examination for these jobs.

Diabetes is an illness that affects how the body absorbs sugar. It can be controlled but not cured. Many people with diabetes have to take an injection of insulin medicine every day. The insulin helps the body absorb sugar. Sonia needed an injection of insulin every morning.

At age seven, Mami taught Sonia how to boil the needle to give herself an injection of insulin. Sonia injected herself each morning before going to school. She learned to be self-reliant at a very young age. She also had to change part of her dream.

Sonia was willing to change her dream, but only a bit. If she could not become a detective like *Nancy Drew*, then becoming a lawyer like *Perry Mason* was the next best job to pursue. When Sonia's relatives asked her what she wanted to be when she grew up, she would always say, "a lawyer." At 10-years old, Sonia *knew* she would go to college and become a lawyer. She never changed her mind. One night, while watching *Perry Mason*, Sonia realized that *Perry Mason* was not the most important person in the courtroom. It was the judge.

The judge was the person who sat majestically in front of the courtroom in black robes. The judge was in charge of the courtroom. The judge controlled when the court session started and when the court session ended. Sonia liked being in charge. She decided she would become a judge *after* she became a lawyer.

Unfortunately, if you were female, it was not easy to become a lawyer or a judge in the 1950s or 1960s, when Sonia was growing up. Most of the judges in the country were male. In fact, at that time, there had never been a woman on the Supreme Court, which was the highest court in the land. Also, there were no Latino or Hispanic justices, like Sonia and her family, on the Supreme Court. Sonia knew it would be hard work to follow her dream of becoming a judge.

CHAPTER 4

Sonia's Good Grades and Hard Work

Sonia wanted to be one of the smartest kids in the class so someday she could become a lawyer and a judge. She and Junior attended Blessed Sacrament Elementary School and Cardinal Spellman High School in the Bronx. They both worked very hard in school and earned good grades.

Sonia's fifth grade teacher gave gold

stars to her students as a reward for good work. Sonia loved getting gold stars. She studied very hard and earned many of them. Whenever Sonia did not know something, she asked for help. She always followed the advice her teachers gave her.

While Sonia was in elementary school, her parents spoke only Spanish at home. Sonia and Junior were bilingual in school. English was their second language. Sonia knew that if she wanted to become a lawyer, she would have to argue cases in court. To do this, she had to learn to speak English very well. To improve her English and practice speaking to groups, Sonia volunteered at her local church. In church, she read the sermons aloud on Sunday mornings to the parishioners. Eventually, Sonia not only improved her English, but she also became an excellent public speaker.

CHAPTER 5

Sonia's Life Changes Again

"People who live in difficult circumstances need to know that happy endings are possible."
Justice Sonia Sotomayor

When Sonia was nine years old, and Junior was six, Papi passed away. This event changed many things in Sonia's life. Mami was very sad and spent many hours alone in her room. There were no more fun Saturdays at Abuelita's because she was also too sad.

After Papi passed away, Mami switched her work hours at the hospital from night time to early daytime hours. She left the apartment at 6:00 a.m. each workday. Now she could be with Sonia and Junior when they came home from school. Mami's rules were different than Papi's rules. Sonia and Junior were allowed to speak English at home. Mami also allowed Sonia and Junior to invite friends to their apartment after school. Everyone who came over had to study and do their homework with Sonia and Junior. Mami often cooked for Sonia, Junior, and all of their friends. Sometimes she cooked rice, beans, and pork for dinner.

In the 1970s, Mami moved the family to an apartment in Co-op City. It had many buildings and was the largest housing development in the Bronx. Sometimes, drug pushers and criminals hid behind the stairs of the large buildings. They sometimes were in the hallways. Mami told Sonia and Junior that they would have to use the elevator and come into their apartment right after school. Sonia and Junior always followed Mami's advice. They learned quickly to avoid the dangers of living in such a large apartment complex.

Even though Mami was a single parent, she was able to feed her children and provide them with clothes and toys. But after paying for these things, Sonia's mother did not have much money left to buy any extra items. One day, an encyclopedia salesman rang the doorbell. Mami listened to his sales' talk and bought the entire set of the *Encyclopedia Britannica* from him. She wanted her children to continue getting good grades in school. Mami made payments for several months to purchase the encyclopedias. Then they owned every volume in the huge encyclopedia. Sonia and Junior used the information in the encyclopedia to get good grades in school. Mami worked hard to be sure her children had the opportunity for a good education.

CHAPTER 6

Sonia Is Courageous and Brave

When Sonia was older, she worked at the local hospital. She still had to inject herself with insulin every morning to control her diabetes.

One day while walking to work, Sonia's insulin needle fell to the ground in front of a police officer. The police officer did not know she had diabetes and thought she was doing something wrong.

Sonia was not afraid to speak-up. She told the police officer she had diabetes. She was not using the needle to take illegal drugs. Sonia was able to convince the police officer to talk to her boss at the hospital. She wanted to prove that she had diabetes, and was not using illegal drugs. She needed the needle to inject herself with insulin. The police officer talked to Sonia's boss, and Sonia did not get into trouble. Sonia was brave enough to speak up for herself when she was wrongly accused of something.

When Sonia was in high school, she

joined the school's debate team. Her friend, Ken Moy, helped her learn how to discuss and argue a specific point of view. Debating helped Sonia to continue improving her English. It also taught her how to win an argument, which is something lawyers need to do.

In high school, Sonia also met her childhood sweetheart, Kevin Edward Noonan. Kevin came over after school, and he and Sonia studied together. Kevin was there so often that he was like a second son to Mami.

Sonia knew she needed good grades

to go to college and law school if she wanted to realize her dream of becoming a lawyer and a judge. When Sonia graduated from high school, she had the highest grades in the class. Because of her grades, she earned the honor of being named the class valedictorian.

On Graduation Day, the valedictorian gives a speech to the graduating students, and their family, friends, guests, and teachers in the audience. Sonia was not afraid to give her speech. She was not afraid of speaking in English before a large group of people.

She had worked hard at reading sermons in her local church, and winning arguments on the debating team. Her hard work paid off. After she graduated from high school, she was able to attend Princeton University on a full scholarship.

CHAPTER 7

Sonia Is Closer to Her Dream

Sonia's family had less money than many other families. Going to college and law school is very expensive. Because Sonia had excellent grades, she received full scholarships to not only Princeton University, but also Yale University Law School. Her mother did not have to pay for Sonia to continue her education. Both schools are thought of as being among the best universities in the country.

Sonia sometimes felt uncomfortable at Princeton. There were not many Latino and Hispanic students or professors at Princeton University. She was different from the "typical" Princeton student, who may have come from a wealthier family. Luckily, her friend, Ken Moy was attending Princeton too. Kevin also came to visit her on the weekends. Sonia spent time with other students, who worked to bring more diverse students and faculty to the university. She also participated in activities to encourage the leaders at the university to hire qualified Hispanics as faculty and staff members. Because of her friends, Ken and Kevin, and her work to increase diversity at Princeton, she was not lonely.

At Princeton, Sonia was not afraid to speak up. She received "A" grades on her work all through high school. Therefore, she was surprised when she received her first "C" on a history exam. She asked one of her professors, Dr. Nancy Weiss (Malkiel), why she received a low grade. Dr. Weiss (Malkiel) told Sonia that her paper had the facts, but she had not used them to create a clear argument. Sonia was good at arguing orally on the debate team. She realized she needed to argue clearly in her writing too. Dr. Weiss (Malkiel) was the Chairperson of the History Department, and later she became Dean of the College. Sonia had the courage to ask for advice and support from Dr. Weiss (Malkiel), one of the best professors at Princeton University.

Sonia improved her writing. She did so well at Princeton that at graduation, she received the Pyne Prize. The Pyne Prize is given to Princeton students who display outstanding leadership. It is Princeton's highest award given to an undergraduate college student. Sonia also graduated from Princeton University with the highest grades in her class. She graduated with the distinction of summa cum laude, which means, "with the highest honor."

After she graduated from Princeton in 1976, Sonia married Kevin. They moved into an apartment on the Yale University Campus in New Haven, Connecticut, where Sonia attended law school. When Sonia graduated from law school, she worked very long hours in New York City, while Kevin studied in Princeton, New Jersey. The long distance away from one another made them grow apart.

Sonia and Kevin eventually divorced, and ended their marriage.

CHAPTER 8

Fulfilling the First Part of the Dream

At Yale University, Sonia studied to become a lawyer. Before her graduation, the New York City District Attorney Robert M. Morgenthau came to speak to the Yale University students. Sonia was walking by the room and heard him speak about working for the district attorney's office. She listened very carefully to what he said. When he finished his talk, Sonia went over to talk to him. He asked her what her goals were, and where she would like to work as a lawyer. She gave him a very good answer. She said she was "exploring" her options. Sonia had not decided yet where she would work after graduation, or what type of law she would practice. District Attorney Morgenthau invited Sonia to interview with him at Yale's Career Center the next day. After their interview, District Attorney Morgenthau asked Sonia to meet with him at his New York City office.

All lawyers, who want to practice law in New York State, must pass the New York

State Bar Exam. After Sonia passed the Bar Exam, she was hired in 1980 as an Assistant District Attorney in New York City. She became part of District Attorney Morgenthau's team of lawyers. Sonia worked as an Assistant District Attorney in New York City for four years. Her dream of becoming a lawyer like *Perry Mason* was finally coming true.

As an Assistant District Attorney, Sonia worked long hours. She investigated cases committed by criminals who were sometimes thieves and murderers. Sonia spent a lot of her time with the police and detectives. She often helped find the evidence to prosecute a case and spent many hours each day preparing for her days in court. At last, Sonia was fulfilling her dream. She was following the examples of her childhood role models, *Nancy Drew* and *Perry Mason*.

CHAPTER 9

Sonia Confronts Criminals, Murderers, and Counterfeiters

Sonia tried criminals in court and sometimes pursued them in the oddest ways. For example, working with the police, one time Sonia rode on the back of a police motorcycle chasing counterfeiters who were copying baseball souvenirs. Sonia worked on many criminal cases. At times she wore a bulletproof vest.

One case she worked on involved the "Tarzan Burglar." The Tarzan Burglar used ropes to swing down from the rooftops of tall buildings to commit his crimes. He carried a gun. Sometimes he broke into his victims' apartments by crashing through the windows or walked on narrow planks over airshafts to enter apartments to rob his victims. Unfortunately he murdered three people before the police captured and arrested him. At his trial, Sonia and another prosecutor questioned forty witnesses over four weeks. At the end of the trial,

Richard Maddicks, the Tarzan Burglar, was sentenced to sixty-two years to life in prison.

After working in the District Attorney's office prosecuting dangerous criminals in New York City, Sonia developed a new specialty, catching counterfeiters. For eight years, Sonia worked at the private law firm of Pavia and Harcourt LLP. At Pavia and Harcourt, Sonia learned about many different types of law, such as corporate law, patents, and counterfeiting.

One of the counterfeiting cases

involved fake designer handbags. The counterfeiters were copying very expensive handbags made by the designer, Fendi. The counterfeiters were selling the handbags to customers, who thought they were buying real Fendi designer bags. After helping the police catch the counterfeiters and successfully sending them off to prison, Sonia received an offer to become a partner at her law firm. This was a great honor. Sonia served as a partner at the law firm of Pavia and Harcourt for four years.

While Sonia was at the law firm,

U.S. Senator Daniel Patrick Moynihan from New York noticed Sonia's hard work and talent. Senator Moynihan was the chairperson of a committee that helped find and recommend the best candidates to serve as judges for the Federal District Courts.

CHAPTER 10

Sonia Becomes Judge Sotomayor

The President nominates, and the United States Senate must confirm the nomination before a federal District Court Judge, a Court of Appeals Judge, or a Supreme Court Justice is appointed. Recommending names of people to serve as federal court judges and justices to the President of the United States is an important job.

Senator Daniel Patrick Moynihan was head of the U. S. Senate Committee on the Judiciary. This committee examined the qualifications of candidates who wish to become federal judges. Each federal district court has at least one District Court Judge, who is nominated by the president and confirmed by the U.S. Senate for a lifetime term.

Sonia was asked to fill out an application to become a federal judge. It took Sonia a week to complete the form. It was so long! After filling it out, she received an appointment for an interview with the committee. Fifteen people interviewed her for the job of federal District Court Judge in the Southern District of New York City. The committee members asked many questions but, as always, Sonia was well prepared for the interview.

After the interview, Senator Moynihan, with support from the other U.S. Senator from New York, Senator Alfonse D'Amato, told Sonia the good news. They decided, with the support of the committee members, to recommend her nomination to the President of the

United States. President George H. W. Bush agreed and nominated Sonia to become a federal judge. When she was thirty-seven years old, in November 1991, Sonia was nominated to be a federal District Court Judge. Sonia was then confirmed by a majority of the Senate members.

There are two senators elected from each of the fifty states. At least sixty of the one hundred senators would have to vote "yes" for Sonia to become a federal judge. After much hard work, she had finally achieved her dream of becoming a judge in August 1992. Sonia had the courage and the determination to be the most important person in the courtroom, the judge. Sonia was now Judge Sonia Sotomayor.

CHAPTER 11

Judge Sotomayor's Dream Job

"I hope none of you assumed...that my lack of knowledge of any of the intimate details of your dispute meant I was not a baseball fan. You can't grow up in the South Bronx without knowing about baseball."

Judge Sonia Sotomayor

Judge Sotomayor loved baseball. When she was a child, she watched baseball with her father. He also taught her the rules of baseball. Her childhood home was in the Bronx near Yankee Stadium.

In 1994, the baseball players went on strike for 232 days. The players and the owners of the teams could not agree to talk about the players salaries. Because of the strike, no one could go to a baseball game. Baseball fans were upset. There would be no World Series. The baseball players wanted the owners to go to court, and have the judge decide who was right.

Judge Sotomayor listened to both sides very carefully. She examined all the evidence. Then she made her decision. The owners wanted to limit the baseball players' ability to discuss raises to their salaries. In her written decision, she told the owners they were wrong. Judge Sotomayor, who was a federal District Court Judge in Manhattan at the time, issued a temporary injunction against the owners of the baseball clubs to end the baseball strike. The players were happy, but the owners were not.

If someone loses a case in District Court, they can appeal the judge's decision to the next highest court. The owners appealed Judge Sotomayor's decision. They went to the next highest court, the Circuit Court of Appeals. The owners lost their case again. Judge Sotomayor's decision was not reversed.

The baseball players and the owners finally came to an agreement. A new contract was signed. The fans were happy because they could attend baseball games again. Many people said District Court Judge Sonia Sotomayor saved baseball when she settled the baseball strike. Fourteen years later, in 2009, Justice Sotomayor threw the ceremonial first pitch before the Yankees played the Boston Red Sox in their baseball game at Yankee Stadium in New York.

After six years as a federal District Court Judge, in 1997, Judge Sotomayor was again nominated to be a federal judge. This time, it was to become a judge in the next highest court which was the (U. S. Second) Circuit Court of Appeals. This court hears appeals from the lower court and determines whether the law was applied correctly. A court in the Circuit Court of Appeals has a panel of three judges and does not have a jury. This time, President Bill Clinton nominated her. To be appointed to the Circuit Court of Appeals, Judge Sotomayor's nomination needed to be confirmed again by a vote in the U.S. Senate. Since federal judges hold their jobs for life, the interviewing process is very long.

The senators asked many difficult questions. In fact, the interview lasted several days. Some senators wanted to know why she made decisions in previous cases. They also wanted to know her opinion about some cases that she might decide in the future. Judge Sotomayor answered all their questions to the best of her ability. Finally, the senators voted. Sixty-eight of the ninety-six senators present that day voted to confirm Judge Sotomayor as a judge on the (U.S. Second) Circuit Court of Appeals.

In the years that Judge Sotomayor sat on the (U.S. Second) Circuit Court of Appeals, she heard over three-thousand appeals from the lower courts. She authored nearly 380 majority opinions. Judge Sotomayor was always well prepared. She studied all the facts. She asked questions of the lawyers on both sides of a case. Judge Sonia Sotomayor decided cases with, "integrity, fairness, and the absence of cruelty."

CHAPTER 12

The Supreme Court

The highest court in the land is the Supreme Court. It is part of the federal court system. Sometimes the Supreme Court is the first and only court to hear a case. For example, when there are disputes between the states or disputes arising among ambassadors, the Supreme Court may be the first and only court to hear the case. The Supreme Court also can review the decisions of lower courts. Reviewing a decision of a judge of a lower court is called an appeal. Most of the cases the Supreme Court hears are appeals from lower courts.

A judge that sits on the Supreme Court is called a Supreme Court Justice. Very few judges ever become a Supreme Court Justice. It is a very high honor. There are nine Justices on the Supreme Court. As stated previously, the two lower federal courts are the District Court and the Circuit Court of Appeals. After being heard by judges in the two lower courts, an application can be made for the Justices to hear the case.

The Justices receive approximately seven to eight thousand requests a year to review a case. But they only have time to hear about eighty cases in a year. In order to hear a case, at least four of the nine Justices have to agree to accept a case. If less than four of the Justices agree to accept a particular case, then the case never comes before the Supreme Court Justices.

When Justice David Souter retired, Judge Sonia Sotomayor was nominated by

President Barack Obama to fill the empty seat on the Supreme Court in May 2009. Judge Sotomayor knew that the full Senate would need to vote on confirming her. She wanted the senators to get to know her beforehand on a more personal and one-to-one basis. Judge Sotomayor decided to visit the senators in their offices in Washington, D.C. Unfortunately, she fell and broke her ankle at La Guardia Airport on June 8, 2009, while rushing to catch the plane. She continued onto a flight to Washington to meet with the senators.

Judge Sotomayor really wanted to become a Supreme Court Justice. Despite her broken ankle, she bravely hobbled around Washington in her cast, meeting and visiting with the senators in their offices so they would get to know her.

In 2009, the U. S. Senate Committee on the Judiciary held hearings on Judge Sotomayor's nomination. The Committee members asked her many questions. She answered them to the best of her ability. Judge Sotomayor, as always, was very well prepared. At the close of confirmation hearings, the Committee voted to send the nomination to the full Senate for consideration. The senators in the full Senate debated for several days before voting. Before Judge Sotomayor could become a Supreme Court Justice, at least three-fifths of the one hundred senators (or at least 60 senators) had to vote for her.

At the Senate hearings, she answered questions for three days. Because Judge Sotomayor wanted to become a Justice, she was not going to leave any question unanswered. She answered every single question to the best of her ability. The questions were about cases she heard, decisions she made, and statements she said in the past.

For example, Judge Sotomayor gave a speech on the Berkley University campus. In the speech, she said, "I would hope that a wise Latina woman with the richness of her experiences would more often than not reach a better conclusion than a white male who hasn't lived that life." Her statement apparently offended some of the white male senators. She explained to the senators that a female judge's experiences might provide a different perspective. This is what she meant in the speech given seven years before.

By the time the Senate hearings were over, many people believed that Judge Sotomayor was well qualified. She had experience as a lawyer and as a District Attorney. She previously worked in criminal, corporate, and civil law. She served as a judge on the federal District Court and the federal Circuit Court of Appeals. She also volunteered her time to help poor people in her community in legal matters, and did not charge them for her legal advice.

The senators voted sixty-eight to thirty-one to confirm Judge Sotomayor as a Justice. They agreed with President Obama that she would make an excellent Supreme Court Justice. One senator was absent, so only ninety-nine senators voted. At the age of fifty-five, Judge Sonia Maria Sotomayor became one of the nine Justices on the Supreme Court. She became the third woman to serve on the Supreme Court. She was also the first Hispanic Supreme Court Justice sitting on the highest court in the United States. Justice

Sonia Sotomayor achieved not only her dream of becoming a judge but she was honored for her work by being confirmed as a Justice of the Supreme Court.

When she was a little girl, living near Yankee Stadium, watching baseball games on TV with her father, she probably never dreamed she would be invited to throw out a first pitch.

Sometimes, with hard work, our lives exceed our dreams.

CHAPTER 13

Judge Sotomayor Becomes a Justice

"You cannot value dreams according to the odds of their coming true. Their real value is in stirring within us the will to aspire. That will, wherever it finally leads, does at least move you forward."
                                Justice Sonia Sotomayor

Justice Sandra Day O'Connor was the first woman appointed to serve on the Supreme Court. Until Justice Sandra Day O' Connor's appointment to the Court by President Ronald Reagan in 1981, all the previous Supreme Court Justices had been men.   When Judge Sonia Sotomayor became a Supreme Court Justice, there was only one other woman, Justice Ruth Bader Ginsburg, serving on the Supreme Court.   Justice Sandra Day O' Connor chose to retire when she turned seventy years old.   Supreme Court Justices are appointed to their positions for life. They can serve for life or for as long as they wish to serve.

Justice Sotomayor interprets the laws in her cases according to the United States Constitution.   She thoughtfully struggles with the intersection of principle, integrity, and compassion in her work. She has stated, "the law must work for all or it works for none." In her book, *My Beloved World*, she describes her point of view as, "I have never accepted the argument that principle is compromised by judging each situation on its own merits."

Being a Supreme Court Justice takes much time. Justice Sotomayor has many friends, but sometimes she has little time to see them. One of her friends, Judge Frederic Block, tells a story about her in his book, *Disrobed: An Inside Look at the Life and Work of a Federal Trial Judge.*

Judge Block illustrates Justice Sotomayor's thoughtfulness and kindness. He once mentioned to Justice Sotomayor that a Puerto Rican doorman in his building cried when Justice Sotomayor was nominated to the Supreme Court. The doorman "was so proud to be Hispanic."

Despite her busy schedule, Justice Sotomayor sent a 5x7 photograph of herself in her Supreme Court robes to the doorman. She signed the photograph "with warm regards." Judge Block delivered the photo to his doorman personally, who was so touched, he cried again.

Justice Sotomayor does not only appear in Court. She has given lectures at universities, written a book, and appeared on TV. In February 2012, she appeared on the TV show, *Sesame Street,* in order to decide the *Case of the Broken Chair* and how to fix it. The issue to be decided by Justice Sotomayor concerned a dispute between *Sesame Street Muppets: Baby Bear and Goldilocks.* Goldilocks broke Baby Bear's chair. Justice Sotomayor made a decision. Both parties accepted it.

Baby Bear and Goldilocks would fix the chair together. Goldilocks and Baby Bear glued the chair together working as partners.

Justice Sotomayor appeared again on *Sesame Street* in November 2012. This time, the appearance was with *Sesame Street Muppet, Abby Cadabby*. Justice Sotomayor helped explain the meaning of the word "career." Instead of being a "princess," Abby Cadabby now wants to become a judge like Justice Sonia Sotomayor.

In her book, *My Beloved World,*

Justice Sotomayor gives credit to her family, relatives, and friends for supporting her throughout her career. She admits that her career path and dreams could not have been accomplished without support from many people. She gives special credit to her mother.

Her mother worked two jobs, and studied to become a nurse when the Justice was growing up. Mami served as an example of perseverance and hard work for Justice Sonia Sotomayor to model as a child and as an adult. Justice Sotomayor's life provides evidence that courage, determination to fulfill your dreams, hard work, discipline, and kindness leads to success.

Justice Sotomayor believes that nothing happens by chance. She considers herself very blessed to have realized her dreams. One of her blessings is her intelligence. Albert Einstein once said, "The true sign of intelligence is not knowledge but imagination." Justice Sotomayor was able to imagine a different future for herself despite enormous odds against achieving it. She had courage, stayed focused on her dreams, worked hard, and was kind and caring. This is a model for living a successful life.

United States Court Systems

There is more than one court system. A city, a village, a state, and the federal government can all have separate court systems. Both the federal government and each of the fifty states have court systems. The Constitution and laws of each state establish the rules of that state's court system. Some judges in a state court system are elected in state elections. They serve a specific term of office.

The federal court system has three

levels: district courts (which are the trial courts); circuit courts (which typically have a three-judge panel that hears the appeals of decisions of the district courts); and the Supreme Court of the United States (the final level of appeal in the federal system). Nine Justices sit on the Supreme Court. There are ninety-four federal district courts.

The President of the United States nominates federal judges and Supreme Court justices. They are confirmed by a vote in the United States Senate. These judges and justices may hold their position for their entire lives, but sometimes a judge or justice resigns or retires earlier. This is true for all federal judges and justices except magistrate judges, which serve a specified term in office.

For more information about the court system, please see the following websites.

U.S. Courts of the Federal Judiciary

http://www.uscourts.gov/about-federal-courts/educational-resources/about-educational-outreach/activity-resources/supreme-1

This website provides information about

the Federal Court system. It includes educational activities.

Supreme Court Historical Society

http://www.supremecourthistory.org

This website includes information about the history of the Supreme Court, events, interviews, videos, and audio recordings.

Supreme Court of the United States

https://www.supremecourt.gov/

This is the official website of the U.S. Supreme Court. It contains information about the U.S. Supreme Court including the biographies of the current Justices of the Supreme Court. It also provides free public access to court procedures and rules, transcripts of oral arguments, and opinions on cases considered by the Court.

U.S. Courts Website

http://www.uscourts.gov/educational-resources.aspx

This website has resources that explain the structure and processes of the court system. It includes educational resources and activities for students, such as information on the Supreme Court, the

Court of Appeals, and District Courts. The website is maintained on behalf of the Judicial Branch of the U.S. Government.

United States Department of Justice

http://www.justice.gov/usao/justice-101/federal-courts

This website, created by the Department of Justice, contains a very good overview of the federal court system.

At the time of publication, all links were active.

Words To Know

Bilingual - using or able to use two languages especially with equal fluency.

Encyclopedia (Britannica) - a reference work (such as a book, series of books, Web site, or CD-ROM) that contains information about many different subjects, or a lot of information about a particular subject.

Hispanic - coming originally from an area where Spanish is spoken and especially from Latin America; *also*: of or relating to Hispanic people.

Latina - a girl or woman of Latin-American origin living in the U.S.

Latino - a person who was born or lives in South America, Central America, or Mexico, or a person in the U.S. whose family is originally from South America, Central America, or Mexico.

Prosecutor - a lawyer who represents the side in a court case that accuses a person of a crime, and who tries to prove that the person is guilty.

Legal Terms Glossary

The definitions of the legal terms below came from the website of the United States Department of Justice. http://www.justice.gov/usao/justice-101/glossary

Appeal - A request made after a trial, asking another court (usually the Court of Appeals) to decide whether the trial was conducted properly. To make such a request is "to appeal" or "to take an appeal." Both the plaintiff and the defendant can appeal, and the party doing so is called the appellant. Appeals can be made for a variety of reasons including improper procedure and asking the court to change its interpretation of the law.

Court - Government entity authorized to resolve legal disputes. Judges sometimes use "court" to refer to themselves in the third person, as in "the court has read the briefs."

Defendant - In a civil suit, the defendant is the person complained against; in a criminal case, it is the person accused of the crime.

Evidence – All relevant information presented in testimony or in documents that is used to persuade the fact finder (judge or jury) to decide the case.

Issue - (1) The disputed point in a disagreement between parties in a lawsuit; (2) To send out officially, as in "to issue" an order.

Judge - Government official with authority to decide lawsuits brought before the courts. Judicial officers of the Supreme Court and the highest courts in some states are called Justices.

Magistrate Judges - Judicial officers who assist U.S. district court judges in getting cases ready for trial. They may decide some criminal and civil trials when both parties agree to have the case heard by a magistrate judge instead of a district court judge.

Opinion - A judge's written explanation of a decision of the court. In an appeal, multiple opinions may be written. The court's ruling comes from a majority of judges and forms the majority opinion. A dissenting opinion disagrees with the majority because of the reasoning and/or the principles of law on which the decision is based.

Panel - (1) In appellate cases, a group of judges (usually three) assigned to decide the case; (2) In the jury selection process, a group of potential jurors.

Plaintiff - The person who files the complaint in a civil lawsuit.

Reverse - When an appellate court sets

aside the decision of a lower court because of an error. A remand often follows a reversal. For example, if the defendant argued on appeal that certain evidence should not have been used at trial, and the appeals court agrees, the case will be remanded for the trial court to reconsider the case without that evidence.

Testify - Answer questions in court.

Trial - A hearing that takes place when the defendant pleads "not guilty" and the parties are required to come to court to present evidence. Also, to settle a dispute in a civil matter.

Witness - A person called upon by either side in a lawsuit to give testimony.

Videos About Justice Sotomayor

C-SPAN Video of Highlights of Justice Sotomayor's Confirmation Hearing.

https://www.c-span.org/video/?287810-1/sotomayor-supreme-court-confirmation-hearing-highlights

A confirmation hearing on the nomination of Judge Sonia Sotomayor to the U.S. Supreme Court was held by the Senate Judiciary Committee on July 13-16, 2009.

This video illustrates some of the questions raised by the following Senators: Sessions, Feingold, Graham, Cornyn, Coburn, Feinstein, Kyl, and Franken. Justice Sonia Sotomayor's answers to the Senators are included.

Judge Sotomayor is Nominated by President Barack Obama.

https://www.youtube.com/watch?v=TX4hL 0b3_uc

Judge Sotomayor speaks about her nomination to the Supreme Court, the influences of her family, friends, and the

U.S. founding fathers on her life and work.

Sesame Street (February 8, 2012): "The Justice Hears a Case."

https://www.youtube.com/watch?v=Fizspm IJbAw

Supreme Court Justice Sotomayor settles a case between Baby Bear and Goldilocks.

Sesame Street (November 9, 2012): Justice Sonia Sotomayor and Abby.

https://www.youtube.com/watch?v=EHICz 5MYxNQ

Supreme Court Justice Sonia Sotomayor gives Abby career advice.

Supreme Court Justice Sonia Sotomayor Visits Yale.

https://www.youtube.com/watch?v=8ODna FRc_mM

Justice Sonia Sotomayor visited Yale University on February 3, 2014. She shared stories about her life with an audience of students, faculty, and staff.

Justice Sotomayor speaks at San Jose State's Student Union Ballroom

https://www.youtube.com/watch?v=98dahk lPTcg

During the October 20, 2014 event, Justice

Sotomayor shared stories about her passion, the law, and stories of her life. Her talk focused on helping others, particularly young people. "You have to have some idealism to go into lawyering. You have to want to help people," said Supreme Court Justice Sonia Sotomayor.

Other Websites

In Profile: U.S. Supreme Court Nominee Sonia Sotomayor

http://www.cbc.ca/world/story/2009/05/26/f-sotomayor.html

This website provides information on Justice Sonia Sotomayor's nomination and a link to her confirmation hearing.

The Website of New York Times

http://www.nytimes.com/interactive/2000/05/26/us/politics/20090526_SOTOMAYOR_TIMELINE.html?_r=0

This is an interactive website. It includes a

timeline, photos, primary sources, and videos of important milestones in Justice Sonia Sotomayor's life.

Lecture: 'A Latina Judge's Voice.'

http://www.nytimes.com/2009/05/15/us/politics/15judge.text.html?pagewanted=all&_r=0

Court of Appeals Judge Sonia Sotomayor delivered the Judge Mario G. Olmos Memorial Lecture at the University of California, Berkeley, School of Law, in 2001. The text of the lecture was published in the Spring 2002 issue of Berkeley La Raza Law Journal, in a symposium issue entitled *"Raising the Bar: Latino and Latina Presence in the Judiciary and the Struggle for Representation."*

At the time of publication, all links were active. You can access the websites by typing the URL into your Web Browser.

References

Block, Frederic. *Disrobed: An Inside Look at the Life and Work of a Federal Trial Judge.* Eagan, Minnesota: Thomson Reuters Westlaw, 2012.

The book describes the life and trials of Federal District Court Judge Frederic Block, whose bench sits in New York City. The book explains, in practical terms, the perspective behind some of the most newsworthy and sensational cases that occurred within the last twenty years.

Gitlin, Martin. *Sonia Sotomayor: Supreme Court Justice*. Edina, Minnesota: Abdo Consulting Group Inc., 2011.

This young adult book for students in grades 7 and up traces Justice Sonia Sotomayor's life from growing up in the Bronx to her appointment as a Supreme Court Justice.

Jackson, Gail Patrick. (Executive Producer). *Perry Mason* [TV]. United States. CBS Television in association with Paisano Productions, 1957.

This TV series ran from September 21,

1957 to May 22, 1966. The series consisted of 271 episodes that portrayed court room scenes. It was based on the written fictional work of writer, Earle Stanley Gardner.

Keene, Carolyn. *Nancy Drew Mystery Series.* **New York, NY: Grosset & Dunlop, Inc., 1930.**

A series of chapter books for children about a girl detective who solved mysteries by searching for clues. Carolyn Keene was the name given to the ghost writers that wrote the 30 books in the series.

McElroy, Lisa Tucker. *Sonia Sotomayor: First Hispanic U.S. Supreme Court Justice*. Minneapolis, Minnesota: Lerner Publications Company, 2010.

Justice Sonia Sotomayor's life is described from her childhood up to her nomination to the Supreme Court including her family, schools she attended, and her career.

Sotomayor, Sonia. *My Beloved World*. New York, NY: Alfred A. Knopf, 2013.

Justice Sotomayor's autobiography, *My Beloved World*, gives more information and detail about her childhood, college days, marriage, friends, family, and her beloved Puerto Rico – the land of her ancestors and Latina heritage. The book contains photographs of the Justice and her family members.

Winter, Jonah. *Sonia Sotomayor: A Judge Grows in the Bronx (la juez que crecio en el Bronx).* **New York, NY: Antheneum Books for Young Readers, 2009.**

This is a picture book for children ages 4 through 8 years old. The life and career of

Justice Sonia Sotomayor are described both in English and Spanish texts. The book includes colorful illustrations by Edel Rodriquez.

Teacher Resources

Aligning Standards, Curriculum, and Assessment: Teaching US History Using Supreme Court Cases. See the following on YouTube.

https://www.youtube.com/watch?v=GkUX Qj8KWu0

In this short video, a teacher talks about using the cases from the Supreme Court in moot court reenactments with his high school class.

Common Core State Standards

This non-fiction book can be used as a resource to implement the Common Core Standards in English/Language Arts. The following are suggested standards Key Ideas for grades 4 through 6 that may be aligned with concepts presented in this book.

Key Ideas and Details: Grade 4

CCSS.ELA-Literacy.RI.4.1

Refer to details and examples in a text when explaining what the text says explicitly and when drawing inferences from the text.

CCSS.ELA-Literacy.RI.4.2

Determine the main idea of a text and explain how it is supported by key details; summarize the text.

CCSS.ELA-Literacy.RI.4.3

Explain events, procedures, ideas, or concepts in a historical, scientific, or technical text, including what happened and why, based on specific information in the text.

Key Ideas and Details: Grade 5

CCSS.ELA-Literacy.RI.5.1

Quote accurately from a text when explaining what the text says explicitly and when drawing inferences from the text.

CCSS.ELA-Literacy.RI.5.2

Determine two or more main ideas of a text and explain how they are supported by key details; summarize the text.

CCSS.ELA-Literacy.RI.5.3

Explain the relationships or interactions

between two or more individuals, events, ideas, or concepts in a historical, scientific, or technical text based on specific information in the text.

Key Ideas and Details: Grade 6

CCSS.ELA-Literacy.RI.6.1

Cite textual evidence to support analysis of what the text says explicitly as well as inferences drawn from the text.

CCSS.ELA-Literacy.RI.6.2

Determine a central idea of a text and how it is conveyed through particular details; provide a summary of the text distinct from personal opinions or judgments.

CCSS.ELA-Literacy.RI.6.3

Analyze in detail how a key individual, event, or idea is introduced, illustrated, and elaborated in a text (e.g., through examples or anecdotes).

About The Authors

Dr. Dolores T. Burton

Dr. Dolores T. Burton is an educator and author. *A Story of Courage: Supreme Court Justice Sonia Sotomayor* is Dr. Burton's fifth book. She co-authored two books for teachers and parents; *The Complete Guide to RtI: An Implementation Toolkit,* (2011) and *Mathematics, the Common Core, and RtI: An Integrated Approach to Teaching in Today's Classrooms* (2013). Her children's picture books, *But You Don't Look Like Me* and *Bully Billy is Back! The Burrowing Owls*

Are Worried, teach lessons of kindness and the acceptance of differences between individuals using owl characters.

Dr. Burton retired as a chair of teacher education and professor at New York Institute of Technology. She received two Fulbright Senior Scholar Awards to assist universities in South Africa and Iceland. She is a former teacher and school district administrator. Throughout her career, she has focused on creating opportunities for all students to obtain academic success.

The Complete Guide to RtI: An Implementation Toolkit (2011), and Mathematics, the Common Core, and RtI: An Integrated Approach to Teaching in Today's Classrooms (2013) were co-authored with Dr. John Kappenberg.

Signed copies of her books and resources for teachers, parents, and children about instructional strategies, owls and bullying are available on www.doloresburton.com and Breaklightpublications.com. More information about her books follows.

The Complete Guide to RTI: An Implementation Toolkit, offers a comprehensive array of strategies for monitoring student progress. Technology and print resources for introducing Response to Intervention (RTI) in a classroom are included. Each chapter has an annotated list of online resources to further study on the topics presented. Chapters include: progress monitoring, instructional support teams, mathematics, literacy, positive behavior supports, collaboration and working with families, information for school and district administrators implanting a RtI program, and building time for RTI in the middle and high school. Paperback is available from www.doloresburton.com and Amazon.com. The book is available on Kindle and Nook from Amazon.com and BarnesandNoble.com.

Mathematics, the Common Core & RTI: An Integrated Approach to Teaching in Today's Classroom by Dolores Burton and John Kappenberg intergrates the central elements of the Common Core and RTI into a single manageable instructional strategy to help all children succeed academically. It provides real-world vignettes and classroom-ready activities for teachers and parents. Chapters include research-based strategies for teaching math vocabulary, English Language Learners, inclusion classes, working with parents, and working with assessment data to increase student success. Available in paperback from www.doloresburton.com, Amazon.com and BarnesandNoble.com. Available on Kindle and Nook from Amazon.com and BarnesandNoble.com.

But You Don't Look Like Me! is a picture book that tells the story of Owlivia, a barn owl, who is lonely. While flying over her new home, she sees a colony of burrowing owls, She flies down to meet them and introduces herself. Because she looks different, the other owls do not like her.

Soon, a scary hawk threatens to carry off Chloe, a baby burrowing owl. Owlivia bravely chases him away while the other owls watch in horror. The owls thank Owlivia for her help, and they become friends even though she doesn't look like them. The story builds on the theme that sometimes good friends can look different from our other friends and us and features the benefits of random acts of kindness. The paperback book is available from www.doloresburton.com, Amazon.com, and breaklightpublications.com. A Read-A-Long DVD containing soundtracks of the book in both English and Spanish is available from www.doloresburton.com, and breaklightpublications.com.

Bully Billy Is Back! The Burrowing Owls

Are Worried is the story of Manny, a small Burrowing Owl, who has difficulty learning new things. Bully Billy watches him struggle and sees opportunities to be a bully. While making fun of Manny, Bully Billy is injured. Later, Manny sees Bully Billy in danger. He performs an act of kindness by flying to get help from Owlivia, a brave, strong Barn Owl. Owlivia then leads all the owls out of danger as she did in *But You Don't Look Like Me!* Bully Billy is saved and changes his mind about being a bully. He realizes that it is better to be a friend than a bully. Resources for parents and teachers about bullying are included. The book is available on www.doloresburton.com, breaklightpublications.com, Amazon.com, and barnesandnoble.com.

Dr. Patricia Ann Marcellino

Dr. Patricia Ann Marcellino is a Professor Emeritus and a former Associate Dean of Academic Affairs at the Ruth S. Ammon School of Education at Adelphi University in Garden City, Long Island, New York. While at the Ammon School of Education, Dr. Marcellino also served as the Director of a Nationally Accredited Leadership program. Dr. Marcellino also worked as the Assistant Dean at Adelphi's Schools of Business. She has experience in the career areas of both business and education, and as an urban New York City, and suburban public school social-studies teacher.

Dr. Marcellino is the author of academic publications and book chapters in national and international venues. Her academic publications have focused on leadership, team-building, career development, and the diversity of learning, especially when implementing *Learning Pattern Theory* and the *Let Me Learn Process* developed by Dr. Christine Johnston. Her work appears in the *Sage Encyclopedia of Educational Leadership and Administration, Volumes 1 & 2.*

Dr. Marcellino was an invited contributor to Dr. Burton and Dr. Kappenberg's book, *The Complete Guide to RTI: An Implementation Toolkit.* She contributed the chapter entitled, *The Role of District and School Administrators in Implementing RTI,* based on her work in leadership development.

For several years, Dr. Marcellino

served as a Trustee and Board Member of the largest Community College in New York State, Nassau Community College.

In addition, Dr. Marcellino has written numerous career articles emphasizing diversity and equality in the workplace for such publications as: *African-American Career World, Careers & The Disabled, Career Woman, Equal Opportunity, Minority Engineer, WD Workforce Diversity,* and *Woman Engineer.* Her articles have focused on developing leadership, communication, and presentation skills, as well as career development in the areas of accounting, banking, business, fashion, management, marketing, nursing, sales, and technology.

Dr. Marcellino is not only the co-author of *A Story of Courage: Supreme*

Court Justice Sonia Sotomayor, she is also the author of: *I Don't Want To Be A Leader: Or Do I?*

I Don't Want To Be A Leader: Or Do I? is an e-book about a girl hesitating to run for Class President because of the negativity she observes in the media regarding presidential elections. Ashlee, the heroine, doubts her leadership abilities, and whether she has the time or the inclination to take on such a demanding role. In a series of conversations through digital formats (text, cell-phone & face-to-face), Ashlee interacts with her various family members and friends until she finally makes a decision about her leadership capabilities and her career direction.

I Don't Want To Be A Leader: Or Do

I? includes 100 activities for parents to develop with a student at home (or home-schooled), and teachers, librarians, and school administrators to adapt in a class, workshop, school or district setting. It's like getting two books in one! Historical events are depicted, and female and male leaders are displayed, among them, Susan B. Anthony, the Blackwell sisters, Lucy Burns, Alexander Hamilton, Senator Robert Kennedy, Rosa Parks, Alice Paul, President Ronald Reagan, Eleanor Roosevelt, Presidential Cousins Franklin Delano and Theodore Roosevelt, Lucy Stone, and Harriet Tubman – to name just a few.

Not only is *I Don't Want To Be A Leader: Or Do I?* based on historical events and role models, it is also based on current events including the recent presidential election of 2016. More importantly, it illustrates how students can run a positive election campaign if they run for class office. *I Don't Want To Be A Leader: Or Do I?* is linked to National Literacy and Social Studies Standards. It is offered exclusively on *Amazon,* and is available on *Kindle HD with Audio.*

ISBN: 978-0-9980927-4-4.

A review by the Director of P.E.A.C.E. July 21, 2016 follows:

I Don't Want to be a Leader: Or Do I? Is a delightful read that connects with children across gender lines and cultural experiences. As a read aloud or individual narrative, children will enjoy the spirited exchange between a young girl and her grandmother exploring reasons why everyone should have opportunities to practice and develop leadership skills. The follow up questions and accompanying resources are especially helpful in giving direction to reflective discussions with students. Our students loved it!

Made in the USA
Middletown, DE
19 September 2018